ON THE MOVE

PLANES

**For a free color catalog describing Gareth Stevens'
list of high-quality books and multimedia programs,
call 1-800-542-2595 (USA) or 1-800-461-9120 (Canada).
Gareth Stevens Publishing's Fax: (414) 225-0377.
See our catalog, too, on the World Wide Web:
http://gsinc.com**

Library of Congress Cataloging-in-Publication Data

Stickland, Paul.
    Planes / Paul Stickland.
       p. cm. — (On the move)
    Includes index.
    Summary: Introduces, in brief text and illustrations, various
types of airplanes and their uses.
    ISBN 0-8368-2153-X (lib. bdg.)
    1. Airplanes—Juvenile literature. [1. Airplanes.] I. Title.
II. Series.
TL547.S824   1998
629.133'34—dc21   98-3351

This North American edition first published in 1998 by
Gareth Stevens Publishing
1555 North RiverCenter Drive, Suite 201
Milwaukee, Wisconsin 53212 USA

© 1991 by Paul Stickland. Produced by Mathew Price Ltd.,
The Old Glove Factory, Bristol Road,
Sherborne, Dorset DT9 4HP, England.
Additional end matter © 1998 by Gareth Stevens, Inc.

Gareth Stevens series editor: Dorothy L. Gibbs
Editorial assistant: Diane Laska

Printed in Hong Kong

1 2 3 4 5 6 7 8 9 02 01 00 99 98

ON THE MOVE

PLANES

Paul Stickland

Gareth Stevens Publishing
MILWAUKEE

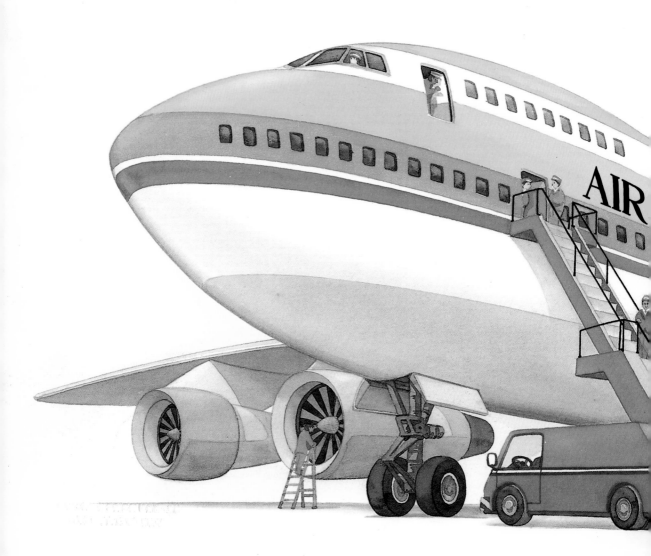

A jumbo jet is one of the largest airplanes in the world. It carries many passengers and needs a lot of fuel.

An ultralight is the smallest airplane.
It can be made from a kit at home.

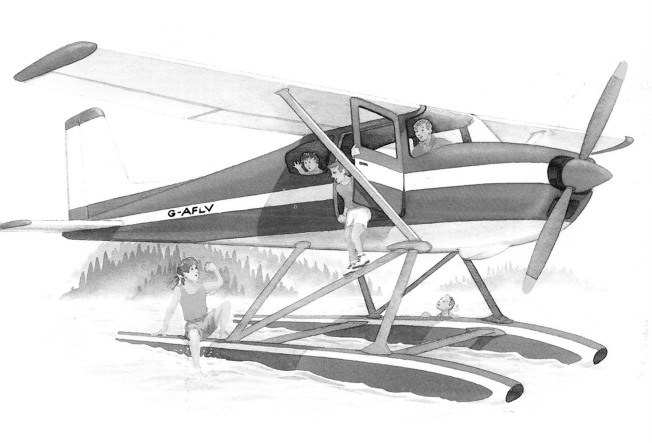

A seaplane can take off and land only
on water.

The Concorde is the fastest passenger
airplane in the world. It has four huge
jet engines hiding under its wings.

If you ride in an old-fashioned biplane,
don't forget your scarf and goggles!

A twin-engine plane can take off
from a very short runway.

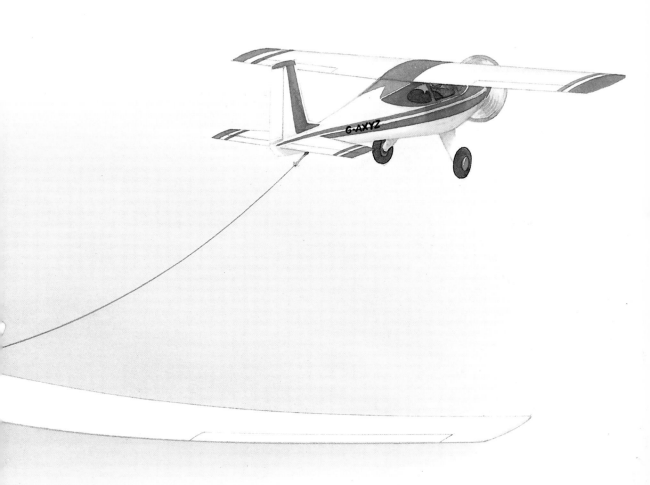

A glider does not have an engine.
A small plane tows it into the sky until
it is high enough to sail off on its own.

Jets are very fast. Pilots can fly some kinds of jets close together in beautiful patterns across the sky.

GLOSSARY

fuel — a solid or liquid material, such as gas, oil, coal, and wood, that makes power or heat when it is burned.

glider — an airplane without an engine or fuel that is towed into the sky where it can fly on currents of air.

goggles — special glasses that fit close to the face around the eyes to keep out wind, dirt, and other harmful things.

kit — a group of parts and pieces that can be put together to make or build something.

runway — a clear path, like a road, that airplanes use to take off and land.

tow — to pull something with a rope or a chain of some kind.

INDEX